# Angel

CW01623610

## Harnessing Divine Power for Holistic Harmony

By

Dr. Prakash Ramchandani

*To the Divine Light within: May this book illuminate the path of healing and spiritual growth for all who seek it.*

# Preface

Angel Reiki is a thread that weaves together ancient wisdom and celestial energies in our life. As we embark on this transformative journey, we are at crossroads—a convergence of earthly practices and ethereal guidance.

For the light workers, Angel Reiki is the next luminous step to explore beyond the familiar pathways of Usui and Karuna Reiki, opening portals to unseen realms.

## Why Angel Reiki?

Angel Reiki is not merely a technique; it is a communion—an embrace of angelic frequencies that resonate with our souls. As we attune to these celestial vibrations, we discover new dimensions of healing, compassion, and spiritual expansion.

## The Pathway Unveiled

In this book, you'll connect with the guidance of archangels and learn how to ask for their help to find clarity and direction in your life. Angel Reiki bridges the earthly and the divine, allowing us to channel healing energy infused with celestial love.

## What Awaits You

*Expanded Awareness*: Angel Reiki opens up hidden doorways within your being. It encourages you to perceive energy beyond the physical senses, to witness the vibrant flow of light and love in every cell.

*Soul Alchemy*: As you weave angelic threads into your practice, you transmute wounds into wisdom. In Angel Reiki, pain turns into something meaningful, and scars become symbols of strength and beauty.

*Higher Realms*: Beyond symbols and hand positions, Angel Reiki leads you to cosmic realms. Here, you connect with angels and receive their special messages. Your healing touch becomes magical and feels like something out of this world..

*Heart Expansion*: Angel Reiki is heart-cantered. It whispers, "You are divinely held." As you channel angelic energy, your heart expands, embracing both earthly struggles and celestial grace.

## A Call to Light Workers

I extend this invitation to my fellow seekers, practitioners, to embrace Angel Reiki. Let it lift you higher, and its light guide you deeper. May your hands be touched by angels, your heart be cradled by light, and your spirit soar on wings of grace.

Dr Prakash Ramchandani

11-Dec-2020

# Acknowledgments

I express my heartfelt gratitude to the Celestial beings and Archangels who guided me in writing and sharing the wisdom of Angel Reiki. Their presence has illuminated my path, and I am honoured to be a conduit for their healing energy.

I also acknowledge my students, Reiki Masters and practitioners who have dedicated their lives to healing and spiritual growth. Your collective energy resonates within these pages, and I am humbled by your commitment to the well-being of others.

To my family and friends, thank you for your unwavering support. Your encouragement fuelled my determination to bring this book into existence.

Lastly, I appreciate the readers—those who seek solace, transformation, and connection with the angelic realm. May this book serve as a beacon of light on your own holistic journey.

May the angels bless you all abundantly.

With love and gratitude,

Dr Prakash Ramchandani

# Prologue

Have you ever felt a yearning to elevate your Reiki practice, to tap into a deeper wellspring of healing energy? If so, then Angelic Reiki beckons you. This transformative modality, far from being a separate system, acts as a potent amplifier for Usui Reiki and other established forms.

By embracing Angelic Reiki, you will embark on a journey of unparalleled growth, empowering you to achieve remarkable results and witness the miraculous unfold.

This book serves as your comprehensive guide to Angelic Reiki, unveiling its profound potential and equipping you with the knowledge and practice techniques to integrate it seamlessly into your existing Reiki practice. Within these pages, you'll discover a powerful synergy waiting to be harnessed.

While Usui Reiki lays a strong foundation, Angelic Reiki transcends its boundaries. While traditional Reiki channels universal life force energy, often perceived as flowing through the practitioner, Angelic Reiki harnesses the purest form of divine energy directly from the Angelic Realm. The practitioner acts as a conduit, ensuring a potent, unfiltered flow of healing light.

While Usui Reiki attunements are typically performed by a Reiki Master, Angelic Reiki, on the other hand, bypasses human intervention. Attunement occurs directly through your guardian angel, ensuring a deeply personal and potent connection to the angelic realm.

Angelic Reiki thus helps you delves deeper, addressing the root causes of physical, emotional, and spiritual imbalances. It tackles past-life issues, ancestral patterns, and karmic burdens, leading to a more profound and lasting transformation.

This amplified healing potential extends to various Reiki techniques, particularly in Psychic Surgery- where it significantly enhances the effectiveness to remove energetic blockages and negativity from the aura and chakras.

Integrating Angelic Reiki with Usui Reiki or your existing practice creates a beautiful synergy. Imagine a gentle flame of Reiki energy, now fuelled by the boundless radiance of the angelic realm. This potent combination translates to several key benefits. Most importantly, Angelic Reiki heightens your connection to your intuition. This Enhanced Intuition allows you to better understand the client's needs and tailor your sessions for optimal results.

The angelic presence fosters profound relaxation, creating a more receptive state for healing within the client that brings forth miraculous results giving spontaneous healing and accelerated recovery through the amplified energy flow.

By opening yourself to Angelic Reiki, you embark on a transformative journey. This book equips you with the knowledge and practical guidance to understand the core principles and history of Angelic Reiki and master the application of Angelic Reiki symbols and techniques.

Witness the profound impact of Angelic Reiki on your own well-being and the well-being of your clients, once you Integrate Angelic Reiki seamlessly into your existing practice.

Angelic Reiki isn't merely a modality. It is a profound connection to the divine realm, a potent tool for achieving remarkable results in every sphere of your life. It is also a catalyst for your own personal growth as a Reiki healer. Are you ready to unlock its potential?

Turn the page and embark on this extraordinary adventure.

# 1. Introduction to Angel Reiki

## What is Angel Reiki?

Angel Reiki represents a harmonious fusion of two profound spiritual practices: traditional Reiki and angelic guidance.

At its core, Angel Reiki is a gentle yet powerful form of energy healing that draws upon the universal life force energy inherent in Reiki, while simultaneously invoking the benevolent presence and support of angels and archangels. By blending these two sacred realms, practitioners of Angel Reiki access a unique and transformative healing modality that addresses the holistic needs of individuals – physically, emotionally, and spiritually.

In Angel Reiki sessions, practitioners act as conduits for divine healing energies, channelling the pure essence of love and compassion that emanates from both Reiki and angelic realms.

Through gentle touch, intention, and connection with angelic beings, practitioners facilitate the flow of healing energy to recipients, promoting balance, restoration, and inner peace. The presence of angels adds an extra layer of guidance, protection, and wisdom to the healing process, allowing recipients to experience profound shifts and insights on their healing journey.

# History and Origins

The origins of Angel Reiki can be traced back to the traditional practices of Reiki, which were developed by Mikao Usui in Japan during the early 20th century.

Usui's teachings emphasized the use of energy healing techniques to promote physical and spiritual well-being, based on the principle of channelling universal life force energy through the hands. Over time, Reiki spread across the globe and evolved into various forms and lineages, each with its own unique emphasis and approach.

In more recent decades, the integration of angelic guidance and assistance into Reiki sessions emerged as a natural progression for practitioners seeking to deepen their spiritual connections and enhance the effectiveness of healing outcomes.

Drawing inspiration from ancient spiritual traditions and contemporary angelic teachings, practitioners began to explore ways to incorporate the loving presence of angels and archangels into their Reiki practice. This fusion of Reiki and angelic energies gave rise to Angel Reiki as a distinct and potent healing modality, offering practitioners a deeper connection to divine guidance and support in their healing work.

## Purpose and Benefits

At its essence, the primary purpose of Angel Reiki is to facilitate holistic transformation on all levels of being – physical, mental, emotional, and spiritual.

By enlisting the assistance of angels and archangels, Angel Reiki practitioners create a sacred space for healing to unfold, allowing recipients to release energetic blockages, trauma, and limiting beliefs that may be hindering their well-being.

The benefits of Angel Reiki are manifold and far-reaching, encompassing both tangible and subtle shifts in the recipient's life. Physically, Angel Reiki promotes relaxation, alleviate pain, and support the body's natural healing processes. Emotionally, it provides comfort, clarity, and release from emotional burdens and past traumas. Spiritually, Angel Reiki fosters a deeper connection to one's inner wisdom, higher self, and the divine, and paves the way for spiritual growth, insight, and alignment with one's life purpose.

Angel Reiki offers recipients a sense of peace, empowerment, and connection to the loving presence of angels and experience profound shifts in consciousness, expanded awareness, and a renewed sense of wholeness and well-being that reverberates throughout their lives.

# 2. Understanding Energy and Healing

*Your body holds deep wisdom. Trust in it. Learn from it. Nourish it. Watch your life transform and be healthy.*

- *Bella Bleue*

## Basics of Energy Healing

Energy healing is a profound and ancient practice rooted in the belief that all living beings possess an innate energy or life force that flows through them, influencing their health and well-being. This concept, found in various cultures and spiritual traditions worldwide, forms the basis of energy healing modalities. These modalities, including Angel Reiki, aim to restore balance, clear blockages, and strengthen the body's energy system to promote healing and vitality.

The fundamental principle of energy healing is that disruptions or imbalances in the flow of energy within the body can manifest as physical, emotional, or spiritual ailments. By working with the body's subtle energy system, practitioners can address these imbalances and facilitate the body's natural healing processes. Energy healing techniques may involve the laying on of hands, visualization, breath work, sound therapy, and intention setting, among others. The Human Energy System

Central to the practice of energy healing is an understanding of the human energy system, which comprises chakras and the aura. Chakras are spinning wheels or vortices of energy located along the body's central axis, from the base of the spine to the crown of the head. Each chakra corresponds to specific physical, emotional, and spiritual aspects of life and is associated with particular organs, glands, and psychological functions.

The aura, or energy field, surrounds the physical body and extends in all directions. It serves as a protective and reflective shield, absorbing and transmitting energy between the individual and their environment. The aura reflects the state of the individual's physical, emotional, mental, and spiritual well-being, as well as their interactions with others and the world around them.

Understanding the human energy system is crucial for Angel Reiki practitioners, as it provides a framework for understanding the energetic dynamics of healing. By working with the chakras and aura, practitioners can identify imbalances, clear blockages, and restore harmony to the energy system, facilitating healing on all levels of being.

## How Angel Reiki Differs from Traditional Reiki

While traditional Reiki and Angel Reiki share fundamental principles and techniques, Angel Reiki incorporates the additional element of angelic guidance and assistance. In traditional Reiki, practitioners channel universal life force energy through their hands to promote healing. In Angel Reiki, practitioners also invoke angels and archangels to enhance the healing process and deepen spiritual connections.

The presence of angels adds a dimension of divine love, wisdom, and protection to Angel Reiki sessions, amplifying the healing energies and guiding practitioners in their work. Angel Reiki symbols, which incorporate angelic imagery and intentions, are used to channel angelic energies and facilitate communication with angelic beings.

Moreover, Angel Reiki practitioners may receive intuitive guidance and messages from angels during healing sessions, providing insights and support for recipients. This collaborative approach between practitioners, recipients, and angelic beings fosters a profound sense of connection, trust, and empowerment, leading to transformative healing experiences.

# 3. Angels of Angel Reiki

In the realm of Angel Reiki, practitioners often invoke the assistance and guidance of divine beings known as angels. These celestial entities are believed to be messengers of the divine, emanating profound love, healing energy, and wisdom.

Each angel possesses unique qualities and attributes, and they play a significant role in the practice of Angel Reiki.

## Hierarchy of Angels

Angels are commonly organized into a celestial hierarchy, each serving specific functions and responsibilities within the divine order. While there are variations in angelic hierarchies across different spiritual traditions, one of the most widely recognized classifications is based on the teachings of various mystical texts and spiritual literature.

1. Archangels: These are considered to be the highest-ranking angels, occupying a position of great authority and power. Archangels are often invoked for protection, guidance, and spiritual assistance.

2. Angels: Angels are divine messengers tasked with carrying out the will of the divine. They are believed to be ever-present guardians, offering comfort, support, and inspiration to those in need.

3. Guardian Angels: Every individual is believed to be assigned a guardian angel at birth. These angels are dedicated to watching over and guiding their charges throughout their lives, offering protection and encouragement along the way.

## Angels of Angel Reiki

In Angel Reiki, practitioners work closely with specific angels, harnessing their divine energy to facilitate healing and spiritual growth. Some of the most commonly invoked angels in Angel Reiki include:

**Figure 1: Archangel Michael with Red flaming sword and shield**

**Archangel Michael**: Known as the protector and defender, Archangel Michael is often invoked for courage, strength, and spiritual cleansing. His presence is associated with the symbol of a sword, representing his ability to cut through negativity and provide divine protection.

**Figure 2: Archangel Raphael, the divine healer**

**Archangel Raphael**: Archangel Raphael is known as the divine healer and protector. His presence is believed to bring comfort, guidance, and healing energy. As the angel of healing and well-being, Archangel Raphael is revered for his ability to bring forth physical, emotional, and spiritual healing. Practitioners often invoke his presence using the symbol of a caduceus, symbolizing his healing energies.

**Figure 3: Archangel Gabriel- associated with communication**

**Archangel Gabriel**: Often depicted as a messenger, Archangel Gabriel is associated with communication, creativity, and guidance. Invoking Archangel Gabriel can help individuals find clarity, inspiration, and purpose in their lives.

**Archangel Uriel**: Regarded as the angel of wisdom and enlightenment, Archangel Uriel is invoked for guidance, intuition, and spiritual illumination. The symbol associated with Archangel Uriel is often depicted as an open hand, representing his willingness to offer guidance and insight.

**Figure 4: Archangel Uriel: Angel of wisdom and enlightenment**

# Invocation and Symbols

In Angel Reiki, practitioners utilize specific symbols to connect with the energies of the angels and channel their healing vibrations. These symbols serve as focal points for intention and invocation, facilitating a deeper connection with the divine realms.

To invoke the presence of an angel in Angel Reiki, practitioners typically follow a ritualistic process that involves meditation, visualization, and the drawing of angelic symbols. These symbols act as conduits for divine energy, allowing practitioners to channel the healing power of the angels into their healing sessions.

For example, to invoke Archangel Michael, practitioners may visualize his radiant presence and draw the symbol of his sword in the air or on the body of the recipient. This symbol serves as a beacon, calling forth the protective energies of Archangel Michael to safeguard and cleanse the individual's aura.

Similarly, invoking Archangel Raphael may involve visualizing his healing light and drawing the symbol of the caduceus to facilitate physical and emotional healing. Through the power of intention and the use of angelic symbols, practitioners can establish a sacred connection with the angels, inviting their divine assistance into the healing process.

In Angel Reiki, angels are revered as powerful allies on the path to healing and spiritual transformation. Through the invocation of specific angels and the use of sacred symbols, practitioners can tap into the boundless love, wisdom, and healing energies of the divine realms. By working in harmony with the angels, practitioners can facilitate profound healing experiences that nurture the body, mind, and spirit.

# 4. Connecting with Angels

## Introduction to Angels and Archangels

Angels, celestial beings of light, exist beyond the physical realm, serving as messengers and assistants in the spiritual realm. These benevolent entities are often depicted as radiant beings emanating pure love and divine wisdom.

Archangels, in particular, hold significant roles in the celestial hierarchy, being high-ranking angels with specific attributes and responsibilities. Each archangel is associated with distinct qualities, such as healing, protection, guidance, and divine justice.

In Angel Reiki practice, understanding and connecting with angels and archangels are foundational. They play an integral role in facilitating healing and spiritual growth. By invoking their presence and assistance, practitioners harness their divine energies to amplify the healing process and receive guidance on their spiritual journey.

The identification and understanding of angels within the context of Angel Reiki draw upon a rich tapestry of spiritual traditions, mystical texts, and divine revelations. Throughout history, various religious and mystical traditions have provided insights into the existence and nature of angels, shaping the beliefs and practices surrounding their invocation and utilization in healing modalities like Angel Reiki.

One of the most influential sources for understanding angels is the Abrahamic religious tradition, which includes Judaism, Christianity, and Islam.

In these traditions, angels are depicted as celestial beings who serve as messengers, intermediaries, and agents of divine will. Sacred texts such as the Hebrew Bible, the Christian New Testament, and the Quran contain numerous references to angels, detailing their roles, attributes, and interactions with humans.

Additionally, mystical texts and spiritual literature from traditions such as Kabbalah, Sufism, and Christian mysticism offer deeper insights into the hierarchy, attributes, and functions of angels. For example, in Kabbalistic teachings, angels are seen as emanations of divine energy, each representing a different aspect of the divine. Similarly, Sufi mystics explore the angelic realm as intermediaries between the divine and the human, embodying qualities such as love, compassion, and wisdom.

In the context of Angel Reiki, practitioners often draw upon these diverse sources of knowledge and inspiration to identify and work with specific angels.

While there is no singular authoritative source for angelic lore within Angel Reiki, practitioners may rely on personal intuition, spiritual guidance, and traditional teachings to establish connections with the angels and integrate their healing energies into their practice.

Through meditation, prayer, and inner exploration, practitioners deepen their understanding of the angelic realm, forging profound bonds with these celestial beings as they journey along the path of healing and spiritual awakening.

## Methods for Connecting with Angels

There are numerous methods to connect with angels, each catering to different preferences and inclinations.

**Meditation** is a powerful tool for quieting the mind and opening oneself to receive angelic guidance. Through meditation, practitioners can create a sacred space within themselves to commune with angels, fostering a deep sense of connection and receptivity.

**Prayer** is another potent method for establishing a connection with angels. By offering heartfelt prayers, practitioners express their intentions, gratitude, and requests for assistance to the angelic realm. This act of devotion and surrender opens channels of communication, inviting angels to respond with love and support.

**Visualization** techniques allow practitioners to create vivid mental images of angels, inviting their presence into the mind's eye. By visualizing angels surrounding and enveloping them in their loving embrace, practitioners strengthen their connection and attunement to angelic energies.

**Intuitive communication** is a direct and personal method of connecting with angels. By quieting the mind and tuning into their inner guidance, practitioners can receive messages, insights, and inspiration from angels. This intuitive exchange often occurs through subtle impressions, feelings, or inner knowingness.

Additionally, practitioners may incorporate external tools such as ***angel oracle cards, crystals, or sacred rituals*** into their practice to deepen their connection with angels. Oracle cards serve as conduits for receiving angelic messages and guidance, while crystals hold vibrational frequencies that resonate with angelic energies. Sacred rituals, such as lighting candles, burning incense, or creating altars dedicated to angels, provide tangible focal points for invoking their presence and blessings.

## Other Angels

In addition to the prominent archangels like Michael, Raphael, Gabriel, and Uriel, Angel Reiki practitioners may invoke a variety of other angels for specific purposes related to healing, guidance, protection, and spiritual growth.

While the selection of angels may vary among practitioners based on personal beliefs, intuition, and the needs of the individual receiving healing, here are a few examples of other angels commonly invoked in Angel Reiki and their associated purposes

**Archangel Metatron**: Known as the angel of sacred geometry and spiritual transformation, Archangel Metatron is often invoked to facilitate spiritual growth, inner wisdom, and alignment with divine purpose.

**Figure 5: Angel Metatron- Sacred Geometry & Spiritual Transformation**

Practitioners may call upon Metatron to help individuals navigate through spiritual challenges, gain clarity, and connect with higher realms of consciousness.

2. **Archangel Ariel**: As the angel of nature and manifestation, Archangel Ariel is revered for her connection to the Earth and her ability to support abundance, prosperity, and environmental healing.

**Figure 6: Archangel Ariel: The angel of nature and manifestation**

Practitioners may invoke Ariel to nurture a deeper connection with nature, attract blessings, and cultivate a sense of harmony and balance in life.

3. **Archangel Chamuel**: Known as the angel of love and relationships, Archangel Chamuel is often invoked to heal emotional wounds, foster self-love, and strengthen connections with others.

**Figure 7: Archangel Chamuel: The angel of love and relationships**

Practitioners may call upon Chamuel to help individuals heal relationships, find inner peace, and open their hearts to unconditional love.

4. **Archangel Zadkiel**: As the angel of forgiveness and mercy, Archangel Zadkiel is revered for his ability to transmute negative energy into love and compassion.

**Figure 8: Archangel Zadkiel: The Angel of Forgiveness and Mercy**

Practitioners may invoke Zadkiel to release past hurts, forgive oneself and others, and experience healing on emotional and spiritual levels.

5. **Guardian Angels**: In addition to specific archangels, Angel Reiki practitioners may also work closely with the guardian angels assigned to individuals at birth. These guardian angels offer personalized guidance, protection, and support throughout life's journey, helping individuals navigate challenges, make wise decisions, and fulfill their spiritual potential.

Each angel invoked in Angel Reiki serves a unique purpose and offers distinct qualities and energies to support healing and spiritual growth. By working in harmony with these celestial beings, practitioners can create sacred spaces for healing, empowerment, and divine intervention, fostering profound transformations in the lives of those they serve.

## Building a Relationship with Angelic Guides

Building a relationship with angelic guides is a journey of trust, openness, and receptivity. Practitioners cultivate these qualities through regular spiritual practices, such as meditation, prayer, and contemplation. By quieting the chatter of the mind and attuning to the subtle whispers of angelic guidance, practitioners deepen their connection with their angelic guides over time.

Developing intuition is the key to building a meaningful relationship with angelic guides. Practitioners learn to trust their inner guidance and discern the subtle nudges and insights offered by angels.

Through practices such as journaling, dream work, and reflection, practitioners enhance their intuitive abilities and strengthen their bond with their angelic guides.

Regular communication with angelic guides is essential for nurturing the relationship. Practitioners can engage in heartfelt conversations with angels, sharing their joys, concerns, and aspirations. By expressing gratitude and trust in the guidance received, practitioners affirm their partnership with angels and invite further support and blessings into their lives.

Connecting with angels is a sacred and transformative practice that enriches the journey of Angel Reiki practitioners. By embracing diverse methods of connection and cultivating a deep relationship with angelic guides, practitioners open themselves to receive divine guidance, healing, and love, empowering them to fulfill their soul's purpose and highest potential.

# 5. Angel Reiki Principles

## Core Principles of Angel Reiki

Angel Reiki operates on a foundation of profound principles, each reflecting the essence of divine love, compassion, and intervention.

At its heart, Angel Reiki practitioners embrace the belief in the inherent goodness that resides within all beings, recognizing the potential for positive transformation through the channeling of divine healing energies. These energies, drawn from the universal source, hold the power to heal and uplift, transcending physical, emotional, and spiritual barriers.

Central to Angel Reiki practice is the principle of honoring free will, acknowledging the sovereignty and autonomy of each individual.

Practitioners understand that healing can only occur when individuals willingly open themselves to receive divine intervention and assistance. Furthermore, practitioners recognize the interconnectedness of all life, understanding that every being is intricately woven into the fabric of existence. This interconnectedness underscores the importance of compassion, empathy, and respect in all interactions, fostering a sense of unity and harmony.

In alignment with divine guidance, Angel Reiki practitioners dedicate themselves to serving as conduits for healing energies, allowing the divine to work through them for the highest good of all.

By embodying these core principles, practitioners cultivate an environment of trust, safety, and unconditional love, paving the way for profound healing and spiritual growth.

## Ethical Considerations and Responsibilities

Practicing Angel Reiki necessitates a deep commitment to ethical conduct and responsible caregiving. Practitioners adhere to a set of ethical guidelines designed to prioritize the well-being and autonomy of clients, fostering an environment of trust and respect.

Central to these guidelines is the principle of obtaining informed consent, ensuring that clients are fully aware of the nature of the healing session and have the freedom to participate voluntarily.

Maintaining confidentiality is paramount in Angel Reiki practice, as practitioners honor the sacred trust bestowed upon them by clients. Practitioners safeguard the privacy and confidentiality of all client information, refraining from disclosing sensitive details without explicit consent. Additionally, practitioners respect the cultural and spiritual beliefs of clients, recognizing and honoring the diversity of individual paths and perspectives.

Practitioners also assume responsibility for their own energy, intentions, and conduct during healing sessions, recognizing the profound impact of their presence on the energetic exchange.

By maintaining a state of purity, integrity, and alignment with divine guidance, practitioners ensure that their actions uphold the highest standards of ethical conduct, fostering an environment conducive to healing and transformation.

## Creating a Sacred Space for Healing

Central to Angel Reiki practice is the creation of a sacred space imbued with divine presence and energy, serving as a sanctuary for healing and spiritual renewal.

Practitioners approach the process of space creation with reverence, intentionality, and mindfulness, infusing every aspect with divine love and light.

*Setting clear intentions* is the first step in creating a sacred space, as practitioners articulate their intentions for healing, protection, and divine intervention. Intentions serve as energetic anchors, guiding the flow of healing energies and aligning the space with the highest vibrations of love and compassion.

*Cleansing and purifying the environment* are essential to remove any stagnant or discordant energy that may hinder the healing process. Practitioners may utilize various cleansing techniques, such as smudging with sacred herbs, sound healing with bells or chimes, or energetic clearing through visualization and intention.

*Invoking the presence of angels and divine energies* is a central aspect of creating a sacred space for Angel Reiki practice. Practitioners call upon angelic beings and divine guides to bless and consecrate the space, infusing it with their loving presence and support. Symbols, rituals, and sacred objects may be employed to amplify the connection with angelic realms and establish a nurturing environment conducive to healing and spiritual growth.

Creating a sacred space for healing in Angel Reiki practice is a sacred and intentional process, guided by the principles of love, compassion, and divine intervention. By honoring these principles and infusing every aspect of space creation with intentionality and reverence, practitioners cultivate an environment of healing, transformation, and divine grace.

# 6. Angel Reiki Symbols and Their Meanings

## Introduction to Angel Reiki Symbols

Symbols are revered as potent conduits of divine energy, each imbued with profound significance and intention.

These symbols, depicted as intricate geometric shapes and designs, serve as vessels for specific energies, qualities, and intentions, facilitating the flow of healing energies during sessions. Rooted in ancient wisdom and spiritual tradition, these symbols are revered as sacred tools of transformation and illumination.

## Their Significance and Usage in Healing Sessions

Angel Reiki symbols enhance healing and divine guidance, guiding practitioners and recipients on a journey of spiritual awakening and renewal.

Each symbol possesses its own unique vibration and purpose, resonating with specific aspects of the human energy system and the angelic realms.

During healing sessions, practitioners harness the power of symbols to focus and amplify healing energies, facilitating profound shifts on physical, emotional, and spiritual levels. By visualizing, drawing, or tracing symbols in the air or on the client's body, practitioners activate their healing properties, initiating a sacred exchange of energy and intention.

These symbols ae the portals to higher realms of consciousness, enabling practitioners to access angelic assistance and wisdom for the highest good of all. Whether used to clear energy blockages, balance chakras, or invoke angelic protection and guidance, Angel Reiki symbols serve as potent catalysts for transformation and healing.

## Drawing and Activating Angel Reiki Symbols

Learning to draw and activate Angel Reiki symbols is an art form steeped in reverence and devotion, requiring practitioners to attune to the subtle nuances of energy and intention.

Through guided practice and meditation, practitioners cultivate a deep connection to each symbol, allowing its essence to flow effortlessly through their being.

Activating symbols involves more than mere physical drawing; it is a sacred ritual of intention-setting and invocation, inviting the assistance of angels and divine guides to amplify their healing effects.

Practitioners use symbols with their thoughts and prayers, and become channels for divine love and healing, channelling the transformative power of the angelic realms into the present moment.

Through this sacred practice, practitioners facilitate profound healing and spiritual evolution for themselves and others.

Angel Reiki symbols are the sacred keys that unlock the doorways to higher realms of consciousness and healing. By working with these symbols with reverence, intention, and devotion, practitioners tap into the limitless reservoir of divine love and wisdom, creating pathways for healing, transformation, and spiritual illumination.

## Symbols used in Angel Reiki, other than Usui Reiki symbols

In Angel Reiki, practitioners utilize a variety of symbols to connect with the energies of angels and facilitate healing, guidance, and spiritual transformation. While some of these symbols may overlap with those used in traditional Usui Reiki, Angel Reiki incorporates additional symbols specifically tailored to work with angelic vibrations. Here are some examples of symbols commonly used in Angel Reiki

1. Angel Wings: Symbolizing protection, guidance, and divine intervention, angel wings are often visualized or drawn by practitioners to invoke the presence of angels in healing sessions. These wings serve as a symbol of the

angelic realm, enveloping individuals in a cocoon of love, light, and divine grace.

2. Halo: Representing purity, enlightenment, and spiritual illumination, the halo is a sacred symbol often associated with angels and divine beings. Practitioners may visualize or draw halos around themselves or their clients to invoke the angelic qualities of purity, clarity, and transcendence.

3. Star: Symbolizing hope, inspiration, and divine guidance, the star is a powerful symbol often used in Angel Reiki to connect with the celestial realms. Practitioners may visualize or draw stars to channel angelic energies, awaken intuition, and navigate through challenges with grace and wisdom.

4. Heart: Representing love, compassion, and healing, the heart is a central symbol in Angel Reiki used to invoke the nurturing energies of the angels. Practitioners may visualize or draw hearts to open the heart chakra, foster self-love and acceptance, and facilitate emotional healing and forgiveness.

5. Spiral: Symbolizing transformation, growth, and evolution, the spiral is a sacred symbol often used in Angel Reiki to facilitate spiritual awakening and alignment with divine purpose. Practitioners may visualize or draw spirals to release old patterns, activate dormant potentials, and journey inward towards self-realization and enlightenment.

6. Dove: Representing peace, purity, and divine blessings, the dove is a beloved symbol in Angel Reiki used to invoke the gentle energies of angels. Practitioners may visualize or draw doves to bring forth a sense of serenity, harmony, and grace into healing sessions, fostering deep relaxation and inner peace.

These symbols, along with traditional Usui Reiki symbols, serve as focal points for intention, visualization, and invocation in Angel Reiki practice. By working with these sacred symbols, practitioners can deepen their connection with the angelic realm, channelling its healing energies to facilitate profound transformations in the lives of those they serve.

# 7. Angel Reiki Techniques

## Grounding and Cantering Techniques

In the practice of Reiki, grounding and cantering techniques serve as foundational pillars, anchoring practitioners in the present moment and establishing a harmonious connection with the Earth's energy.

Through visualization, breath work, or physical exercises, practitioners cultivate a deep sense of rootedness and stability, grounding themselves in the nourishing embrace of Mother Earth.

**Figure 9: Visualisation and Grounding**

Visualization techniques involve envisioning roots extending from the base of the spine deep into the Earth, anchoring the practitioner firmly to the ground.

Breath work practices focus on deep, intentional breathing, drawing in vital life force energy and releasing tension and distractions with each exhale.

**Physical exercises**, such as Yoga, mindful walking, ad gentle exercises encourage practitioners to embody their connection to the Earth, feeling the support of the ground beneath their feet with each step.

**Figure 10: Physical exercises and Grounding**

By grounding, practitioners create a solid energetic foundation from which to channel healing energies and facilitate transformative healing experiences for themselves and others.

# Cleansing and Balancing the Energy Field

As in Usui Reiki, cleansing and balancing the energy field are essential steps in Angel Reiki too. Practitioners can employ other techniques too, each as unique as the individual practitioner, to purify and harmonize the aura and chakras, the subtle energy centres of the body.

**Scanning** techniques involve sweeping the hands or a crystal pendulum through the energy field, detecting areas of congestion or imbalance and bringing them into conscious awareness. Sweeping motions help to disperse stagnant or negative energy, allowing the natural flow of healing energy to be restored.

**Smudging**, the burning of sacred herbs such as sage is another powerful technique used to cleanse and purify the energy field, dispelling negativity and creating a sacred space for healing to occur. As the smoke wafts through the air, practitioners visualize it carrying away any unwanted energies, leaving behind a sense of clarity and renewal.

Balancing techniques focus on redistributing energy flow within the aura and chakras, promoting harmony and vitality on all levels of being.

By directing healing energy with focused intention and gentle touch, practitioners facilitate the release of energetic blockages and the restoration of balance and wholeness.

Through these sacred practices, practitioners honour the innate wisdom of the body and spirit, creating pathways for healing, transformation, and spiritual evolution to unfold.

## Hands-on Healing Methods with Angels

Angel Reiki utilises hands-on healing technique, in partnership with angels. The practitioners serve as conduits for the flow of healing energy, as guided by the angels.

During hands-on healing sessions, practitioners may employ a variety of techniques, ranging from light touch to hovering gestures, as they work in tandem with angelic beings to amplify and direct the flow of healing energy.

Light touch techniques involve placing the hands lightly on or near the body, allowing the gentle transmission of healing vibrations to permeate the recipient's being.

Hovering gestures, where the hands are held a few inches above the body, enable practitioners to work with the subtle energy field surrounding the physical body, accessing deeper levels of healing and transformation.

Visualizing angelic presence during hands-on healing sessions invokes the loving support and guidance of angels, enhancing the healing process and fostering a profound sense of peace and wholeness.

As practitioners open themselves to the divine flow of healing energy, they become vessels of love and compassion, offering solace and support to those in need.

With each healing session, practitioners and recipients alike are enveloped in the gentle embrace of angelic presence and experience the divine love and grace.

# 7. Angel Reiki Attunements

## Understanding Attunements in Angel Reiki

Attunements serve as sacred rites of passage in the practice of Angel Reiki, administered by Reiki Masters to initiate practitioners into the realm of Angel Reiki.

These rituals orchestrate a harmonious alignment between the practitioner's energy field and the frequencies of Angel Reiki symbols and energies. Through this process, practitioners' receptivity to channelling healing energy and connecting with angelic beings is heightened, facilitating profound healing experiences.

## Preparation for Receiving Attunements

Before undergoing an attunement, practitioners engage in preparatory rituals to cultivate readiness and openness.

This preparatory phase often involves cleansing practices to purify the physical and energetic bodies, meditation to quiet the mind and centre the spirit, and setting intentions to align with the principles and energies of Angel Reiki. Practitioners approach the attunement process with humility, surrendering to the divine flow and embracing the transformative energies that await them.

## Performing Attunements for Others

Reiki Masters trained in Angel Reiki hold the sacred responsibility of conducting attunements for others seeking to deepen their connection to Angel Reiki energies.

Attunements may be administered in person or remotely, following a prescribed protocol to ensure the integrity and efficacy of the process.

During the attunement ceremony, practitioners infuse recipients with Angel Reiki energies, guiding them through a profound initiation into the mysteries of divine healing.

Reiki Masters also offer guidance and support to recipients as they integrate the attunement energies into their practice, nurturing their growth and evolution as healers.

# 8. Conducting an Angel Reiki Session

## Setting up the Healing Space

Creating a conducive environment lays the foundation for an effective Angel Reiki session.

Practitioners begin by purifying and energizing the healing space, using techniques such as smudging or sound healing to clear stagnant energies and invoke sacred presence.

Comfortable seating or a massage table is arranged to promote relaxation and receptivity, while sacred objects or symbols may be placed strategically to enhance the healing atmosphere.

By infusing the space with love and intention, practitioners create a sanctuary where clients can experience profound healing and transformation.

## Client Consultation and Intention Setting

Prior to commencing the session, practitioners engage in a client consultation to understand the client's needs, concerns, and aspirations for healing.

Through active listening and compassionate communication, practitioners establish rapport and trust, co-creating a safe container for healing to unfold.

Together, practitioners and clients collaboratively set clear intentions for the session, aligning their energies and intentions to facilitate the highest good. This dialogue fosters a sense of empowerment and partnership, ensuring that the healing process honours the client's unique journey and aspirations.

## Step-by-Step Guide to an Angel Reiki Session

Angel Reiki sessions follow a structured yet intuitive format, tailored to meet the specific needs and energies of each client.

1. The session typically begins with grounding and cantering exercises to establish a strong energetic foundation.

2. This is followed by aura cleansing and chakra balancing techniques to clear blockages and restore balance.

3. Practitioners then channel healing energy with the assistance of angels, using hands-on or hands-off techniques to transmit divine love and light to areas of need.

4. Throughout the session, practitioners remain attuned to the client's energy and intuition, adjusting their approach as guided by divine wisdom.

5. Integration techniques are employed to seal the healing process, leaving clients feeling nurtured, uplifted, and aligned with their highest potential.

# 9. Self-Care and Maintenance

## Importance of Self-Care for Practitioners

Practitioners of Angel Reiki recognize the importance of prioritizing self-care to sustain their health, vitality, and spiritual well-being.

Self-care practices encompass a holistic approach to wellness, including regular meditation, Reiki self-treatments, physical exercise, nourishing nutrition, restorative rest, and seeking support from mentors or peers.

By nurturing themselves with love and compassion, practitioners replenish their energetic reserves and cultivate resilience in the face of life's challenges.

## Techniques for Self-Healing with Angel Reiki

Angel Reiki offers practitioners powerful tools for self-healing and personal growth, empowering them to address physical, emotional, and spiritual imbalances within themselves.

Self-healing practices may include hands-on healing with angelic assistance, visualization techniques, affirmations, and meditation with angelic guidance.

As practitioners deepen their connection to Angel Reiki energies, they awaken to their innate wisdom and potential, embodying the healing light of divine love within themselves.

## Maintaining Energetic Hygiene and Balance

Practitioners maintain energetic hygiene practices to cleanse, protect, and replenish their energy field on a regular basis, safeguarding their energetic integrity and well-being.

These practices include aura cleansing to clear stagnant energies, cord cutting to release unhealthy attachments, smudging to purify the energy field, and energy shielding to establish boundaries.

By honouring their energetic boundaries and maintaining balance within themselves, practitioners create a sacred container for Angel Reiki healing to flow freely and authentically.

# 10. Integrating Angel Reiki into Daily Life

## Applying Angel Reiki Principles beyond Healing Sessions

Angel Reiki principles illuminate the path of daily life, fostering spiritual growth, resilience, and alignment with divine guidance.

Practitioners embody mindfulness, gratitude, and compassion in their interactions with others, infusing each moment with the healing energy of divine love.

By integrating Angel Reiki principles into their daily lives, practitioners become catalysts for positive change, radiating light and inspiration wherever they go.

## Manifestation and Intention Setting with Angels

Practitioners harness the transformative power of Angel Reiki energies to manifest their desires and intentions with the assistance of angelic beings.

Through visualization, affirmation, and sacred ritual, practitioners co-create their reality in alignment with their highest good and divine purpose. Angels serve as supportive allies and guides, illuminating the path ahead and empowering practitioners to manifest their dreams with grace and ease.

## Building a Practice and Community

Practitioners of Angel Reiki must share their gifts and talents with the world, offering healing sessions, workshops, and events in their communities.

Building a practice involves networking, marketing, and cultivating relationships with clients and fellow practitioners, creating a supportive ecosystem of mutual growth and collaboration.

By nurturing a vibrant community of like-minded individuals, practitioners amplify their impact and contribute to the collective healing and evolution of humanity.

# 11. Conclusion

## Recap of Key Concepts and Techniques

Angel Reiki represents a sacred journey of healing, transformation, and spiritual awakening, uniting the healing energies of Reiki with the guidance of angels.

Throughout this manual, practitioners have been introduced to foundational principles, techniques, and practices that empower them to deepen their connection to divine healing energies and serve as vessels of love and light in the world.

## Resources for Further Learning and Practice

For those eager to expand their study and practice of Angel Reiki, a wealth of resources awaits, including books, online courses, workshops, and community gatherings.

Practitioners are encouraged to continue their education, seek guidance from experienced teachers, and engage in ongoing self-reflection and growth. With each step along the journey, practitioners deepen their understanding and embodiment of Angel Reiki, enriching their lives and the lives of those they touch.

## Continued Growth

As practitioners embark on their journey with Angel Reiki, they should remember that healing is a sacred dance of self-discovery and integration.

Trust in the wisdom of the heart, the guidance of angels, and the transformative power of divine love. May each moment be a testament to the beauty and grace of the healing journey, inspiring practitioners to shine brightly and share their gifts with the world.

Blessed be!

# Notes

## Symbols used in Angel Reiki and angels that are associated with them

In Angel Reiki, several symbols are commonly used, each with its own unique meaning and associated angels. Here are some of the key symbols used in Angel Reiki and the angels associated with them.

1. The Power Symbol (Cho Ku Rei)

**Figure 11: Power Symbol and associated Angels**

Associated Angels: Archangel Michael, Archangel Gabriel, and Archangel Raphael.

Meaning: The Power Symbol is used to increase the power of healing energy and protection. It is also used to focus energy on specific areas during healing sessions.

2. The Mental/Emotional Symbol (Sei He Ki)

**Figure 12: Emotional Balance Symbol and associated Angels**

Associated Angels: Archangel Chamuel and Archangel Zadkiel.

Meaning: The Mental/Emotional Symbol is utilized to balance emotions, clear negative thought patterns, and promote mental clarity and stability.

3. The Distance Symbol (Hon Sha Ze Sho Nen)

**Figure 13: Distance Symbol and associated Angels**

Associated Angels Archangel Metatron and Archangel Sandalphon.

Meaning: The Distance Symbol enables practitioners to send healing energy across time and space, for distant healing and connecting with past or future events.

4. The Master Symbol (Dai Ko Myo)

**Figure 14: Master Symbol and associated Angels**

Associated Angels: Archangel Uriel and Archangel Jophiel.

Meaning: The Master Symbol represents enlightenment, spiritual growth, and the integration of divine wisdom. It is used to enhance spiritual awareness and deepen the connection with angelic guidance.

## 5. The Angelic Healing Symbols (Shika Sei Ki and Shika So)

Shika Sei Ki and Shika So work in harmony to promote emotional well-being.

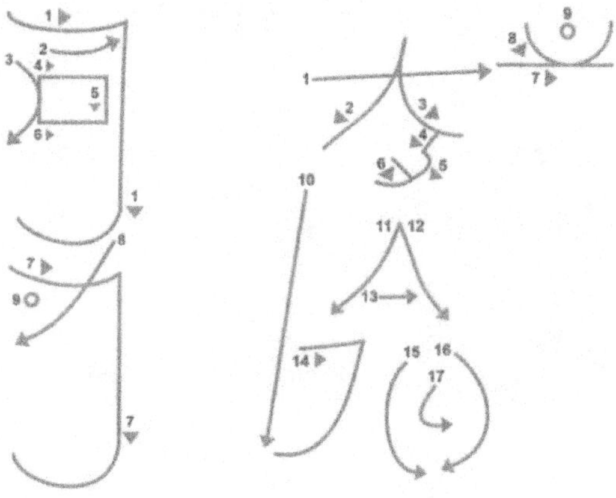

Figure 15:Shika Sei Ki and Shika So

Shika Sei Ki acts as a gentle cleanser, washing away negativity and opening your heart and soul to healing. Shika So then helps fostering a connection between your emotions and your ability to communicate them effectively. Together, they act like a bridge between your inner world and the world around you. This powerful combination allows you to express yourself authentically, fostering stronger, more therapeutic relationships.

Associated Angels: Archangel Raphael, Archangel Azrael, and Healing Angels.

Meaning: The Angelic Healing Symbol invokes the presence of healing angels and facilitates the healing of physical ailments, emotional wounds, and spiritual imbalances.

6. The Harmony Symbol (Raku)

**Figure 16: Harmony Symbol Raku**

Associated Angels: Archangel Raguel.

Meaning: The Harmony Symbol promotes balance, harmony, and alignment with divine grace. It is used to restore equilibrium in relationships, environments, and energetic fields.

Archangel Raguel is known as the angel of justice and harmony. His name means "Friend of God." Raguel works to ensure that justice, orderliness, and fairness prevail in heaven and among human relationships.

These symbols serve as focal points for intention-setting and energy transmission during Angel Reiki sessions, and practitioners may invoke the assistance of the associated angels to amplify their healing effects.

Unlike Usui Reiki, which uses a small set of well-known symbols, Angelic Reiki employs a much larger number of symbols, with some sources mentioning up to 12. These symbols are said to be attuned to the energy of various angels and archangels. However, due to the relatively new and evolving nature of Angelic Reiki, there isn't a universally standardized list of symbols or their angelic associations.

Here are some of the commonly used symbols in Angelic Reiki:

The Atlantean Master Symbol -

**Figure 17: Atlantean Master Symbol**

This symbol is said to connect the practitioner to the energy of the Angelic Realm and the higher aspects of themselves.

The Archangel Michael Shield - This symbol is said to invoke the protective energy of Archangel Michael.

The Archangel Raphael Caduceus - This symbol is said to be connected to the healing energy of Archangel Raphael. The caduceus is a staff entwined with two serpents, commonly used as a symbol of medicine.

It's important to note that Angelic Reiki is not a lineage recognized by the Reiki Usui Shiki Ryoho Gakkai, which is the governing body of Usui Reiki.

## Awakening Angelic Wisdom

Connecting with Angelic Guides- Nurturing Intuition and Connection

### Setting Your Intention

Connecting with angelic guides begins with a sacred intention. In the quietude of your heart, express your desire to commune with these celestial beings. Let your intention be clear and unwavering.

### Creating a Receptive Space

Imagine a tranquil sanctuary—a place where the veil between realms thins. Sit in stillness, breathe, and open your heart. Feel the presence of angelic energies enveloping you. Trust that they hear your call.

### Invoking Their Presence

Speak softly or silently. Address your angelic guides by name or simply as "Beloved Angels." Invite them into your life, your thoughts, and your dreams. Trust that they respond, even if their whispers are as gentle as a breeze.

### Signs and Synchronicities

Angelic communication often arrives through signs. Look for feathers, rainbows, or unexpected encounters. Pay attention to recurring numbers—these are coded messages. Trust your intuition to decipher their meaning.

## Meditation Practices for Angelic Communication

### Heart-Cantered Meditation

Sink into your heart chakra. Visualize it as a radiant sphere of light. Invite angelic energies to merge with your essence. Listen—not with your ears, but with the receptive chambers of your soul.

### Visualizing Angelic Beings

In meditation, step into a sacred garden, a mountaintop, or a celestial temple. There, meet your angelic guides.

Observe their forms, their wings, their eyes filled with cosmic knowing. Engage all your senses.

### Mantras and Affirmations

Repeat angelic mantras "I am open to divine guidance." "Angels, reveal your wisdom." Let these sacred syllables resonate within you. Affirm that you are a vessel for angelic communication.

## Incorporating Angelic Reiki into Daily Life

### Morning Intentions

As dawn breaks, infuse your waking moments with angelic energy. Set intentions for love, healing, and grace. Bless your day, knowing that your angelic companions walk beside you.

### Self-Healing Rituals

Invoke angelic symbols—their geometry holds ancient wisdom. Place your hands on your heart, your brow, your belly. Imagine healing light flowing through you. Trust that you are held by celestial hands.

### Blessing Your Meals

Before each meal, pause. Acknowledge the angels who oversee nourishment. Whisper gratitude. Imagine their blessings infusing your food with vitality and love.

## Rituals and Practices for Self-Healing

### Chakra Clearing

Sit in stillness. Visualize each chakra as a spinning vortex of light. Invoke angelic energy to cleanse and balance them. Trust that your energy centres harmonize with the celestial realms.

### Hands-On Healing

Place your hands where healing is needed. Feel the warmth—the touch of angelic grace. Trust that your intention aligns with theirs. Healing ripples through you like sacred water.

### Angel Cards or Oracle Decks

Draw cards with reverence. Each card carries an angelic message. Reflect on their symbols, their colours. Trust that the cards weave a tapestry of guidance.

## Using Angelic Reiki for Manifestation and Intention Setting

### Clear Intentions

Write your desires on parchment or whisper them to the wind. Be specific. The angels listen. Your intentions are seeds—they sprout in the luminous soil of angelic realms.

### Invoking Angelic Support

Ask your guides to assist. Trust that they orchestrate cosmic alignments. Their wings brush against the fabric of reality, weaving threads of manifestation. Surrender to their divine choreography.

### Visualize and Feel

Close your eyes. See your intention realized. Feel it in your bones, your breath, and your heartbeat. Angelic energy amplifies your visions. You are co-creating with celestial forces.

## Maintaining a Connection with Angelic Energies

### Gratitude Practice

At sunset, stand beneath the sky's canvas. Thank the angels. Their presence is woven into every sunset, every dew-kissed petal. Gratitude opens celestial portals.

### Nature Connection

Walk barefoot on earth's skin. Listen to the rustle of leaves—their secrets whispered by angels. Birds carry messages. The wind carries their breath. You are kin to all creation.

### Dream Journaling

Keep a journal by your bedside. Record dreams—their cryptic language. Angels visit in slumber. Decode their messages. Trust that your dream state bridges realms.

## The Daily Practice Sequence

### Morning Invocation

As dawn paints the sky, stand by your window. Breathe. Set your intention for the day. Invite angel

## Dream Interpretation: Unveiling Hidden Meanings

Dream interpretation is a fascinating exploration of the subconscious mind. Here are additional examples to deepen our understanding:

1. Teeth Falling Out

Symbolism: Teeth symbolize communication, confidence, and vulnerability.

Possible Interpretations:

> Anxiety: Feeling unprepared or exposed.
>
> Loss of Control: Fear of losing influence or power.
>
> Transition: A sign of personal growth or change.

2. Being Chased

Symbolism: Represents avoidance, fear, or unresolved issues.

Possible Interpretations:

Avoidance: Escaping from something you don't want to face.

Emotional Threat: Fear of confronting suppressed emotions.

Life Challenges: Encounters with obstacles or stressors.

3. Flying

Symbolism: Freedom, transcendence, and breaking boundaries.

Possible Interpretations:

Empowerment: Feeling liberated or in control.

Spiritual Ascent: Connection to higher realms.

Escapism: Desire to escape daily constraints.

4. Water

Symbolism: Emotions, intuition, and the subconscious.

Possible Interpretations:

Cleansing: Emotional release or purification.

Navigating Life: Calm waters signify stability; turbulent waters indicate emotional turmoil.

Depth: Exploring hidden feelings or memories.

5. Animals

Symbolism: Animals carry archetypal meanings.

Possible Interpretations:

Cats: Independence, mystery, or feminine energy.

Snakes: Transformation, healing, or hidden knowledge.

Birds: Freedom, messages, or spiritual guidance.

6. Loved Ones Dying

Symbolism: Represents change, transformation, or fear of loss.

Possible Interpretations:

Metaphorical Death: Endings or transitions in relationships.

Grief: Unresolved emotions related to loss.

Symbolic Rebirth: Transformation and renewal.

7. School

Symbolism: Learning, growth, and self-discovery.

Possible Interpretations:

Past Experiences: Reflecting on education or childhood.

Life Lessons: Opportunities for growth and development.

Anxiety: Feeling unprepared or inadequate.

8. Sex

Symbolism: Intimacy, desire, and connection.

Possible Interpretations:

Literal Desire: Reflecting unmet physical needs.

Symbolic Union: Seeking emotional or spiritual connection.

Power Dynamics: Examining relationships and vulnerability.

9. Falling

Symbolism: Loss of control, insecurity, or fear.

Possible Interpretations:

Insecurity: Fear of failure or inadequacy.

Life Changes: Transition or instability.

Letting Go: Surrendering to the circumstances.

Remember, dream interpretation is deeply personal. Trust your intuition, explore recurring themes, and consider the context of your waking life. Each dream is a portal to self-discovery and hidden wisdom.

# Epilogue

As you close this book, a potent energy hums within you – a testament to the transformative power of Angelic Reiki. The journey has undoubtedly been enriching, filled with discoveries about the angelic realm, the profound healing potential, and the personal growth you've experienced.

Remember, Angelic Reiki is not a destination, but a continuous unfolding.

Here are some ways to keep this sacred practice vibrant in your life:

*Maintaining Your Connection:*

Dedicate time daily for quiet meditation or prayer. This fosters a constant dialogue with your guardian angels and the angelic realm, keeping the channel open for angelic guidance and energy flow.

*Practice Makes Perfect:*

Regularly apply Angelic Reiki to yourself, loved ones, and even your environment. Remember, the more you practice, the more comfortable and confident you become, allowing the angelic energy to flow effortlessly.

*Sharing Your Light:*

As your skills and confidence grow, consider sharing Angelic Reiki with others. Offer healing sessions, workshops, or even write about your experiences to inspire others. Remember, the more hearts touched by Angelic Reiki, the brighter the world becomes.

*Continuing Education:*

The field of Angelic Reiki is constantly evolving. Explore additional resources, attend workshops, and connect with other practitioners to broaden your knowledge and deepen your practice.

## Witnessing Miracles

As you continue your journey, remember that miraculous healings are not extraordinary events; they are the natural outcome of aligning yourself with the boundless power of the angelic realm. Embrace these miracles with gratitude, not astonishment. Let them fuel your passion and inspire you to reach out and heal even more deeply.

## A Note of Gratitude

This book would not exist without the guidance of the angelic realm and the countless healers who have dedicated themselves to this beautiful practice. May gratitude flow to all who have contributed to the evolution and understanding of Angelic Reiki.

## The Final Page: A New Beginning

As you turn the final page, remember, this is not an ending, but a new beginning. A chapter unfolds, filled with the potential for profound healing, personal growth, and a life illuminated by the radiant light of Angelic Reiki. May your journey be filled with blessings, and may you continue to be a beacon of light in the world.

Farewell, dear reader, and may the angelic blessings be with you always.

# Afterword

As I conclude this journey through the realm of Angel Reiki, I find myself humbled by the profound wisdom and healing potential that this practice offers. Throughout these pages, we have explored the intersection of spiritual energy, angelic guidance, and the innate healing capacities within each of us.

Angel Reiki is not merely a technique or a modality; it is a sacred bond between the divine and the human soul. It is an invitation to surrender to the higher vibrations of love, compassion, and harmony that the angelic realm graciously offers.

In our modern world, where stress, anxiety, and disconnection often prevail, the gentle touch of Angel Reiki serves as a beacon of hope and restoration. It reminds us that amidst the chaos, there exists a sanctuary within ourselves where healing begins.

As you start your own Angel Reiki journey, may you remember that you are not alone. The angels stand beside you, ready to assist and guide you on your path to wholeness. Trust in their presence, and allow their loving energy to flow through you.

Remember, too, that Angel Reiki is a practice of continuous growth and evolution. Just as the universe is ever-expanding, so too is our capacity to channel divine healing energy. Embrace each moment with an open heart, knowing that every experience is an opportunity for learning and transformation.

In closing, I extend my deepest gratitude to the angels who have graced these pages with their wisdom and light. May their blessings accompany you always, guiding you towards a life filled with love, joy, and spiritual abundance.

With love and angelic blessings,

Dr. Prakash Ramchandani

# About the Author

Dr. Prakash Ramchandani is a renowned Reiki Grandmaster, healer, and spiritual teacher with a deep commitment to facilitating healing and a lifelong passion for holistic well-being and spiritual exploration.

With over two decades of experience in the field of energy healing, Dr. Ramchandani has dedicated himself to mastering the intricacies of Reiki and other complementary modalities. As a Reiki Grandmaster, he has not only honed his skills as a practitioner but has also emerged as a respected mentor and guide for aspiring healers. His compassionate and intuitive approach to teaching empowers individuals to tap into their innate healing abilities and cultivate a deeper connection with the universal life force energy.

In addition to his work as a healer and teacher, Dr. Ramchandani has authored several books and articles on Reiki, energy healing, and spiritual growth. His writings are revered for their clarity, depth, and practical insights, offering readers a profound understanding of the spiritual dimensions of healing.

He is committed to spreading the teachings of Reiki far and wide. Through his workshops, seminars, and online courses, he continues to touch the lives of individuals seeking healing, guidance, and spiritual illumination.

With a heart full of compassion and a spirit guided by wisdom, Dr. Prakash Ramchandani stands as a beacon of light in the world of energy healing, inspiring countless souls to embark on their own journey of self-discovery and transformation.

# Other Books by the Author

All books are available on Amazon and Notionpress

Printed in Dunstable, United Kingdom

81488033R00047